D1223172

A First Look at Unicorns

by Emma Carlson-Berne

BUMBA BOOKS™

LERNER PUBLICATIONS ◆ MINNEAPOLIS

To Elise

Note to Educators

Throughout this book, you'll find critical-thinking questions. These can be used to engage young readers in thinking critically about the topic and in using the text and photos to do so.

Lerner Publications Company
An imprint of Lerner Publishing Group, Inc.
241 First Avenue North
Minneapolis, MN 55401 USA

For reading levels and more information, look up this title at www.lernerbooks.com.

Main body text set in Helvetica Textbook Com Roman.
Typeface provided by Linotype AG.

Editor: Andrea Nelson **Designer:** Lauren Cooper
Lerner Team: Katy Prozinski and Martha Kranes

Library of Congress Cataloging-in-Publication Data

Names: Berne, Emma Carlson, author.
Title: A first look at unicorns / by Emma Carlson Berne.
Description: Minneapolis, MN : Lerner Publications, [2021] | Series: Bumba books - fantastic creatures | Includes bibliographical references and index. | Audience: Ages 4–7 | Audience: Grades K–1 | Summary: "Emergent readers will delight in learning about how we imagine unicorns and where stories about them come from through carefully leveled text and a close text-to-image match"— Provided by publisher.
Identifiers: LCCN 2019035052 | ISBN 9781541596818 (library binding) | ISBN 9781541599772 (ebook)
Subjects: LCSH: Unicorns—Juvenile literature.
Classification: LCC GR830.U6 B47 2021 | DDC 398.24/54—dc23

LC record available at https://lccn.loc.gov/2019035052

Manufactured in the United States of America
1-47787-48227-10/15/2019

Table of Contents

Unicorns!

Picture a beautiful white horse with a horn on its head. This is what a unicorn might look like.

Unicorns are not real. But people imagine they are.

People imagine that unicorns hide in forests. They are fast. They are hard to find.

In some stories, unicorns are horses. They have long manes and tails. They have a twisted, pointy horn.

In other stories, unicorns look like goats. They may have tails like lions!

What other animals could unicorns look like?

Real horses do not have

horns on their heads.

But rhinos do.

A whale called a narwhal has a long tooth. The tooth sticks out of its mouth. It looks like a horn.

What other animals have horns?

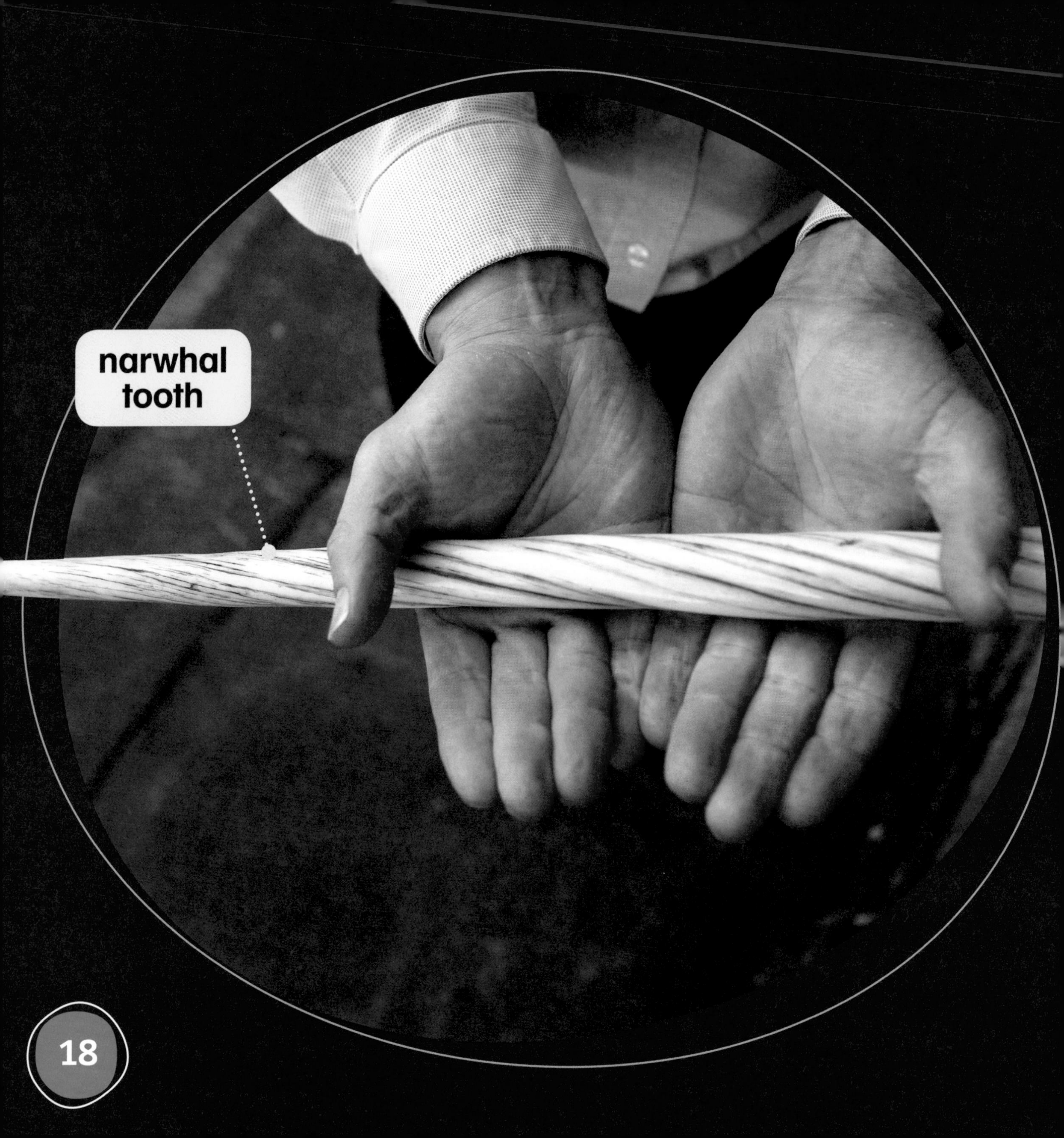
narwhal
tooth

Long ago, people would say rhino horns were unicorn horns. They thought narwhal teeth were unicorn horns.

People thought unicorn horns were magic. They thought the horns would keep them from getting sick.

Unicorns are still magical in our imaginations!

21

Parts of a Unicorn

Picture Glossary

imagine

to picture something in your mind

magical

something not real that is thought to have special powers

narwhal

a whale with a long, pointy tooth sticking out of its mouth

rhinos

large mammals that eat plants and have one or two horns on their noses

Read More

Carlson-Berne, Emma. *A First Look at Mermaids.* Minneapolis: Lerner Publications, 2021.

Editors of DK Publishing. *The Everything Book of Horses and Ponies.* New York: DK Children, 2019.

Sherman, Jill. *Forests and Vegetation.* New York: Enslow, 2018.

Index

Photo Credits

Image credits: Digital Storm/Shutterstock.com, p. 5; Hisham Ibrahim/Getty Images, pp. 6, 23 (top left); Donald Iain Smith/Getty Images, p. 9; CoreyFord/Getty Images, pp. 10, 23 (bottom left); Bettmann/Getty Images, p. 13; Abhishek Singh & illuminati visuals/Getty Images, pp. 14, 23 (bottom right); CoreyFord/Getty Images, p. 17; David Cheskin/PA Images/Getty Images, p. 18; walbyent/Getty Images, pp. 21, 23 (top right); Warpaintcobra/Getty Images, pp. 22.

Cover: ratpack223/Getty Images.